EXPLORING
WEATHER

Scientific Consultants:
Margaret W. Carruthers
Heather Sloan

Photo Credits:
Michael Giudice: page 15
AP/Wide World Photo: pages 19, 27
Tom Bean/DRK: pages 15, 18-19, 21
John Gerlach/DRK: page 18
Johnny Johnson/DRK: pages 24-25
Wayne Lynch/DRK: page 13
S. Nielsen/DRK: page 15
David Smart/DRK: page 23
Larry Ulrich/DRK: page 17
Jeremy Woodhouse/DRK: page 17
Granger Collection: pages 7, 21, 25
FPG International: page 10
Ken Fraser/FPG International: page 29
Keith Gunnar/FPG International: page 25
Alan Kearney/FPG International: pages 5, 24
Harvey Lloyd/FPG International: pages 28-29
Fred McKinney/FPG International: page 25
Diane Padys/FPG International: page 10
Richard Price/FPG International: page 8
J. Robinson/FPG International: page 21
Stephen Simpson/FPG International: pages 18-19
Adam Smith/FPG International: page 10
Robert Srenco/FPG International: page 19
Thayer Syme/FPG International: pages 10-11
Telegraph Colour Library/FPG International: pages 6, 7, 29
VCG/FPG International: end pages; page 13
Wayne Aldridge/International Stock: page 13
Warren Faidley/International Stock: pages 20-21, 27
Faidley/Agliolo/International Stock: pages 6-7
NASA: pages 8-9, 11, 12, 16, 26
NOAA Photo Library: page 28
B & C Alexander/Photo Researchers: page 24
Howard Bluestein/Photo Researchers: page 23
Scott Camzine/Photo Researchers: page 24
Chesher/Photo Researchers: page 22
Jack Fields/Photo Researchers: page 9
Simon Fraser/Photo Researchers: pages 12-13
Michael Gilbert/Photo Researchers: page 11
Leonard Lessin/Photo Researchers: page 28
Damien Lovegrove/Photo Researchers: page 9
Hank Morgan/Photo Researchers: pages 6, 29
NASA/Photo Researchers: pages 16, 27
NOAA/Photo Researchers: page 6
Warren Faidley/Weatherstock: pages 8, 12, 14-15, 21, 22, 26, 28

Illustrations:
Robin Makowski: pages 9, 12, 16, 17, 18, 22

Visit us at www.kidsbooks.com
Volume discounts available for group purchases.

EYES ON ADVENTURE™

EXPLORING
WEATHER

**Written by
Kathy Wilmore**

kidsbooks
Incorporated

WEATHER IS . . .

"Everybody talks about the weather," said Mark Twain, "but nobody does anything about it." There isn't much we can do about the weather—though we have found ways to predict and cope with it. By studying weather, scientists better understand what's going on in the atmosphere. They can inform and prepare people for what may lie ahead—rain and drought, heat waves and snow storms, lightning and thunder, wind, hurricanes, and tornadoes!

WHAT'S UP?

Weather is what is happening in the atmosphere above and around us each day. Weather is different from climate: *Weather* is what happens from day to day; *climate* is the average weather trend over long periods of time.

▲ El Niño causes storms and rough seas worldwide.

GOING GLOBAL

Fishermen in the Pacific near Peru noticed that, every few years, a warm current arrived around Christmastime. They named it El Niño (the boy-child) after the baby Jesus. That current affects weather worldwide. It causes downpours where it's normally dry, drought where it's normally moist, and stronger-than-usual storms.

▼ The dark-red area to the west (left) of South America is the mass of warm water known as El Niño.

◄ FORECAST

Meteorology is the scientific study of the atmosphere and weather. Meteorologists are not just TV news people. Most work behind the scenes, studying wind patterns, temperature changes, and computer models of various conditions. They look for ways to understand, explain, and predict the weather.

Thunderstorms can be so strong that they form violent tornadoes.

SMALL WORLD

You may never set foot anywhere near the Sahara in Africa, but the weather there can still affect you. Desert winds can whip sand into the atmosphere, where it may travel around the world. Dust from the Sahara has been found in London, England, and Chicago, Illinois!

◀ CONTROL FROM ON HIGH

Humans have always tried to understand and explain the weather. At one time, most people believed that weather changes were caused by gods. The Aztecs of Mexico believed that a giant, plumed serpent called Quetzalcoatl (ket-SAHL-kwat-ul) controlled the winds, which brought rain and other kinds of weather.

GREAT BALL OF FIRE!

For thousands of years, human beings have known that the sun plays an important role in the conditions around them. Nearly every early civilization in the world worshiped the sun in some way. What those civilizations may not have known is that the heat that travels to Earth from the sun is what makes weather happen.

HOT STUFF!

You see it every day, but what do you really know about the sun—our closest star?

- **Distance across:** 864,000 miles
- **Speed its light travels:** 186,000 miles per second
- **Temperature at its core:** 27,000,000°F
- **Average distance from Earth:** 92,980,000 miles
- **Temperature at its surface:** 10,000°F
- **Time its light takes to reach Earth:** 8.3 minutes

HOT AND COLD

Ever notice how, on a hot, sunny day, you feel hotter in dark-colored clothes? Earth's surface is like that. Dark areas—rich soil, city streets, and deep-green forests (left)—absorb and hold more heat than light surfaces, such as clouds. Bright, shiny surfaces, such as snow or ice (below), reflect heat away.

Earth in January
(Winter in North America, summer in South America.)

Winter

Summer

SUN

Summer

Winter

Earth in July
(Summer in North America, winter in South America.)

▲ SEASON'S HEATINGS
Earth is tilted as it orbits the sun. When the Northern Hemisphere is tilted toward the sun, it experiences the warm days of summer, while the Southern Hemisphere experiences the cold of winter. The opposite occurs when the north is tilted away from the sun.

ON THE FRONT LINES
The sun's uneven heating of Earth's surface is what makes air move. A warm front is a large mass of warm air, which rises. A cold front is a large mass of cold air, which sinks. When these two meet, look out! The weather is going to change, and it's likely to be wet.

This line of clouds moving across the sky is an approaching front.

TOO HOT TO HANDLE

We may enjoy the warmth of the sun on a mild day, but when weather gets too hot, it can spell trouble. Heat kills more people than any other kind of weather—including hurricanes, tornadoes, and lightning. In 1999, a heat wave killed hundreds of people in the Midwest. A heat wave in 1936, one of the hottest U.S. summers on record, killed 4,678 people.

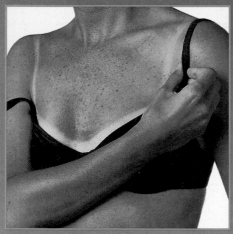

Be careful of too much sun. Painful sunburns cause dehydration and damage to your skin. Just one bad sunburn drastically increases your risk of developing skin cancer later in life.

GETTING STEAMED

High humidity, or lots of moisture in the air, makes you feel hotter than the actual temperature. Why? Sweating is the human body's way of cooling off. In dry air, sweat evaporates. But too much moisture in the air leaves the sweat on your body with no place to go.

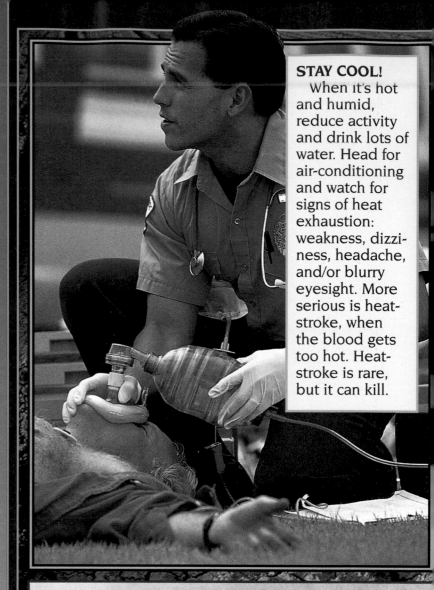

STAY COOL!
When it's hot and humid, reduce activity and drink lots of water. Head for air-conditioning and watch for signs of heat exhaustion: weakness, dizziness, headache, and/or blurry eyesight. More serious is heatstroke, when the blood gets too hot. Heatstroke is rare, but it can kill.

The Dust Bowl of the 1930s was caused by the most famous drought in U.S. history. A sharp decrease in rain on the Great Plains started it. It got worse as the sun made the soil drier, and high winds blew the soil away, often in huge clouds.

BONE DRY
Drought is when an area gets much less rain than usual. Without rain, land will dry out. Droughts often come hand in hand with heat waves, although they occur in cooler weather as well.

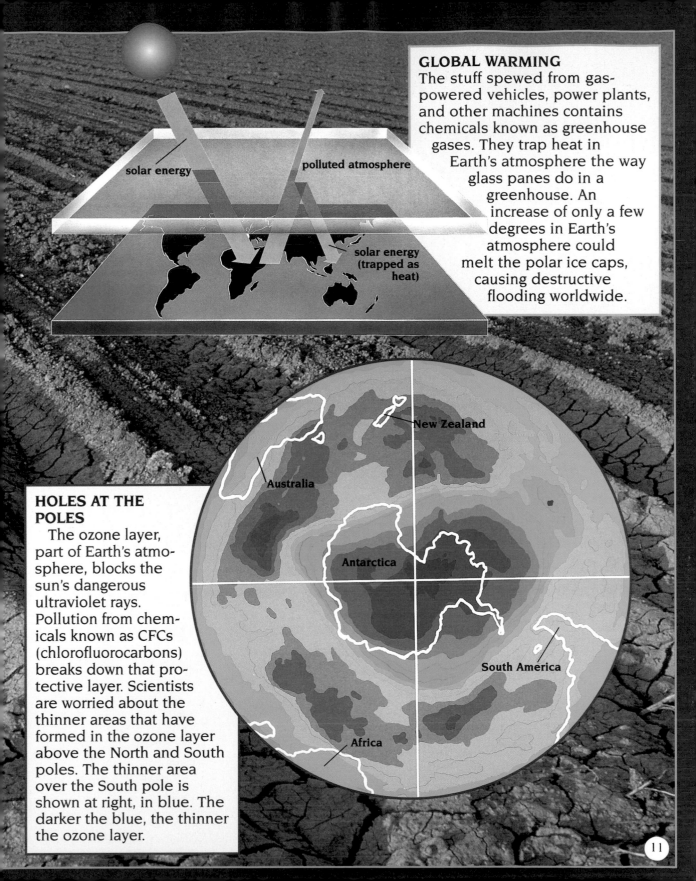

GLOBAL WARMING
The stuff spewed from gas-powered vehicles, power plants, and other machines contains chemicals known as greenhouse gases. They trap heat in Earth's atmosphere the way glass panes do in a greenhouse. An increase of only a few degrees in Earth's atmosphere could melt the polar ice caps, causing destructive flooding worldwide.

solar energy

polluted atmosphere

solar energy (trapped as heat)

HOLES AT THE POLES
The ozone layer, part of Earth's atmosphere, blocks the sun's dangerous ultraviolet rays. Pollution from chemicals known as CFCs (chlorofluorocarbons) breaks down that protective layer. Scientists are worried about the thinner areas that have formed in the ozone layer above the North and South poles. The thinner area over the South pole is shown at right, in blue. The darker the blue, the thinner the ozone layer.

New Zealand

Australia

Antarctica

South America

Africa

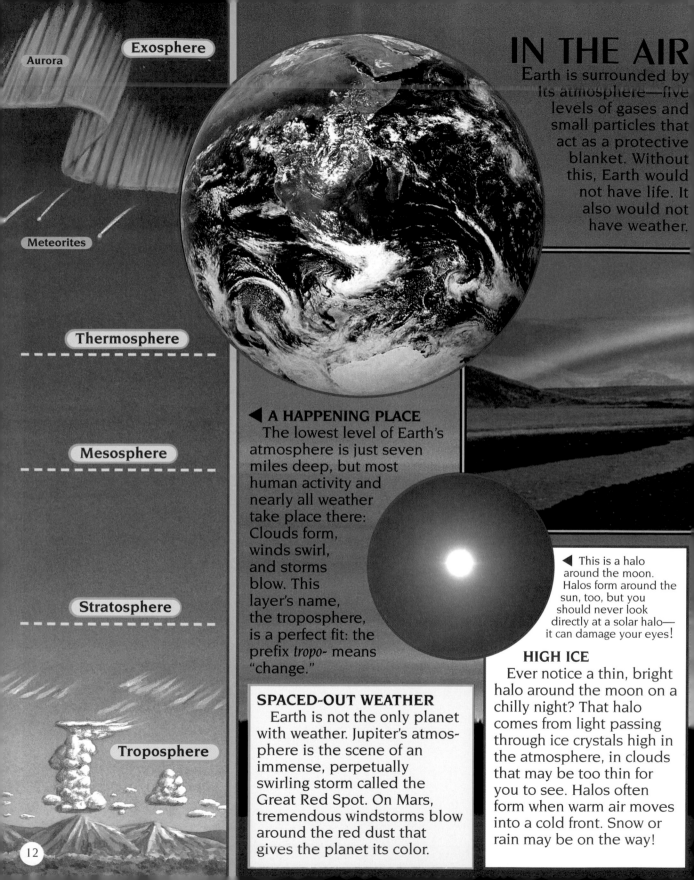

Aurora

Exosphere

Meteorites

Thermosphere

Mesosphere

Stratosphere

Troposphere

IN THE AIR

Earth is surrounded by its atmosphere—five levels of gases and small particles that act as a protective blanket. Without this, Earth would not have life. It also would not have weather.

◀ A HAPPENING PLACE

The lowest level of Earth's atmosphere is just seven miles deep, but most human activity and nearly all weather take place there: Clouds form, winds swirl, and storms blow. This layer's name, the troposphere, is a perfect fit: the prefix *tropo-* means "change."

SPACED-OUT WEATHER

Earth is not the only planet with weather. Jupiter's atmosphere is the scene of an immense, perpetually swirling storm called the Great Red Spot. On Mars, tremendous windstorms blow around the red dust that gives the planet its color.

◀ This is a halo around the moon. Halos form around the sun, too, but you should never look directly at a solar halo—it can damage your eyes!

HIGH ICE

Ever notice a thin, bright halo around the moon on a chilly night? That halo comes from light passing through ice crystals high in the atmosphere, in clouds that may be too thin for you to see. Halos often form when warm air moves into a cold front. Snow or rain may be on the way!

LOVE THAT SUNSET!

Thank the atmosphere for the brilliant red of a gorgeous sunset. When the sun is low in the sky, its light travels a longer distance, through more atmosphere, than it does when the sun is high above. The denser atmosphere blocks nearly all of the shorter light waves. Only longer light waves make it through, displaying reds, oranges, and yellows.

SITTING PRETTY

A rainbow is a combination of sunlight, air, and water. After a shower, the air is dense with water. If the sun breaks through clouds, the light flows through the curved surface of those droplets. That bends the light the way a prism does, breaking it into bands of color.

AIR YOU CAN SEE

When ground-level air gets full of moisture, fog forms. This low-lying cloud can make driving cars, flying planes, or steering ships dangerous. The piercing beam of a lighthouse is one of the few things that can cut through the murk.

KILLER FOGS

In the 1800s and early 1900s, fogs in London, England, made many people ill, some fatally. Sooty particles given off by coal fires and factory smokestacks hung in the damp air, damaging people's lungs. Antipollution measures have made those "killer fogs" a thing of the past.

San Francisco is famous for its fog. The Golden Gate Bridge, which spans San Francisco Bay, is equipped with foghorns to alert the boats sailing beneath it. From July through October (the area's foggiest season) the foghorns sound for five to six hours a day!

THE CLOUD CROWD

Every cloud tells a story—if you know how to read it! There are three basic types. **Stratus** clouds are layered and streaky-looking, with indistinct edges. **Cumulus** clouds are big and puffy-looking, with flat bottoms. **Cirrus** clouds are white and wispy, broad but thin.

Prefixes or suffixes added to stratus, cumulus, and cirrus tell you more about various forms of these types. For instance, *nimbo-* or *-nimbus* means rain. Here are the most commonly seen clouds.

HIGH-LEVEL CLOUDS
The prefix *cirro-* tells you that it's a high-level cloud.

Cumulonimbus
• up to 50,000 feet or higher
• a sign of severe weather—high winds, heavy downpours, thunder and lightning, tornadoes

---

MID-LEVEL CLOUDS
The prefix *alto-* tells you that it's a mid-level cloud.

Altostratus
• 6,000 feet to 20,000 feet
• a sign that a warm front is moving in, bringing a change in the weather (probably rain or snow)

Altocumulus
• 6,000 feet to 20,000 feet
• often lined up in row upon row, making for dramatic sunrises and sunsets; a sign that moisture is on the rise, so rain may follow

---

LOW-LEVEL CLOUDS

Stratocumulus
• below 6,000 feet
• often fill the entire sky; a sign that a storm has ended and skies are clearing

Cumulus
• below 6,000 feet
• a sign of fair weather

Nimbostratus
• below 6,000 feet
• a stratus cloud so dense with water or ice that it blocks out the sun; a sure sign of rain or snow

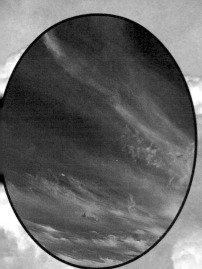

▼ Cirrus
- above 18,000 feet
- form under windy conditions; sometimes form tail-like clouds called "mare's tails," as seen below

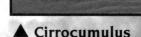

▲ Cirrocumulus
- above 18,000 feet
- has a rippled look to it, sometimes looks like the scales on a fish

Cirrostratus ▲
- above 18,000 feet
- formed from ice crystals; will not block out sunlight, but enough cirrostratus clouds will turn the sky from blue to white

THE LITTLEST CLOUDS
Have you ever noticed that little white puff that appears when you breathe out on a cold day? That cloud formed the same way the big ones form. The air inside your warm body holds a lot of moisture. When you exhale into the cold, that air suddenly cools. The moisture in it condenses and hangs, visible, in the air.

LIGHT AND SHADOW
Sunshine reflecting off water droplets or ice crystals is what makes clouds look white. When light can't pass through—because the water or ice is very dense—a cloud looks dark.

Not every cloud has a silver lining. Those that do have it because the sun is hidden behind the densest part of the cloud, but its light reflects brightly off the thinner area at the edges.

Stratus
- below 6,000 feet
- flat, streaky layers of cloud, turning the sky dull and gray

Fog
- ground level
- often forms at night or early morning, when air is coolest; burns off when sun rises high enough to warm the low-lying air

15

THAR SHE BLOWS!

What causes wind? Ancient peoples thought that it was a powerful god puffing and blowing; today's scientists think more in terms of irregular warming of air by the sun. As warm air rises and cool air sinks, the air moves. We feel that as wind.

THE JET SET ▶

Jet streams are swift, powerful bands of wind that blow in a regular route over long stretches of the planet. They influence climate. One jet stream, which blows from the Caribbean to northern Europe, carries warm air with it, making affected areas well north of the equator warmer and greener than other places nearby.

This line of clouds shows the Northern Hemisphere Jet Stream over eastern Canada.

BEAUFORT SCALE ▼

Weather watchers use the Beaufort scale as a guide to wind speeds. It is named for Sir Francis Beaufort, a British admiral, who devised it in 1805.

North America

New Zealand

South America

THE FORCE IS WITH YOU

The Coriolis force has a tremendous effect on Earth's winds. It comes from the way Earth spins. This spin—always in the same direction—forces winds north of the equator to bend toward the right, and winds south of the equator to bend leftward. That is why a tropical cyclone's winds spin counterclockwise in the Northern Hemisphere, and clockwise in the Southern Hemisphere.

▲ The white lines show the direction of the wind. Can you see the different swirls in the Northern and Southern Hemispheres?

Wind speed (mph): below 1
Description: calm
Effects on land: smoke rises straight up

Wind speed (mph): 2-3
Description: light air
Effects on land: smoke drifts slowly

Wind speed (mph): 4-7
Description: light breeze
Effects on land: leaves rustle; wind vanes move

Wind speed (mph): 8-12
Description: gentle breeze
Effects on land: leaves and twigs move

Wind speed (mph): 13-18
Description: moderate breeze
Effects on land: small branches move; dust flies

Wind speed (mph): 19-24
Description: fresh breeze
Effects on land: small trees sway

SCULPTOR

Wind is one of the most powerful forces on Earth. Like water, it is responsible for shaping landscapes. Over time, wind can carve cliffs, whittle rock formations, and stunt tree growth.

These rock formations in Utah (right) are called *hoodoos*. Thousands of years of wind and blowing sand carved the sandstone into these unique shapes.

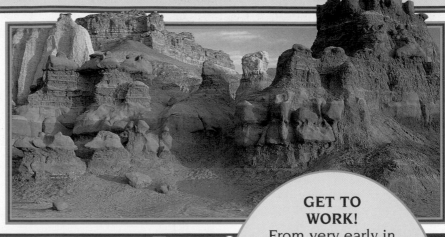

These windmills, which stretch for miles on high, windy ground, generate electricity for part of southern California.

GET TO WORK!

From very early in human history, humans have found ways to make wind work for them. Wind power has been used to propel sailing ships, turn wheels that control water pumps or other machines, generate electricity, and lift planes into the air!

BUNDLE UP! ▶

Why does it feel colder on a windy day? Our bodies give off heat. On a relatively still day, even if it's cold out, some of that heat hangs close by for a little while—but wind whips it away, making us feel colder. Meteorologists call this the wind-chill factor.

WHAT'S THE WIND CHILL?

ACTUAL TEMP.	15 mph wind	20 mph wind	25 mph wind	30 mph wind
30°F	feels 9°F	feels 4°F	feels 1°F	feels -2°F
20°F	feels -5°F	feels -10°F	feels -15°F	feels -18°F
10°F	feels -18°F	feels -24°F	feels -29°F	feels -33°F
0°F	feels -31°F	feels -39°F	feels -44°F	feels -49°F

(If the wind is blowing at 30 miles per hour when it's 15°F out, it will feel like -25°F to your body.)

Wind speed (mph): 25-31
Description: strong breeze
Effects on land: large branches sway; wind "whistles"

Wind speed (mph): 32-38
Description: near gale
Effects on land: whole trees sway; difficult to walk into wind

Wind speed (mph): 39-46
Description: gale
Effects on land: twigs break off trees

Wind speed (mph): 47-54
Description: strong gale
Effects on land: branches break off trees

Wind speed (mph): 55-63
Description: whole gale
Effects on land: trees uprooted; damage done to buildings

Wind speed (mph): 64-74
Description: storm
Effects on land: extensive damage to landscape

Wind speed (mph): above 74
Description: hurricane
Effects on land: major destruction

WATER EVERYWHERE

Water is an essential element of weather. No matter how still it may look in a pool or drinking glass, it is always on the move.

Condensation

Precipitation

Evaporation

Ocean

Lake

◀ NATURE'S RECYCLING

Water in oceans, lakes, and rivers evaporates—turns into vapor and rises into the air. That vapor then condenses to form clouds. When clouds get overloaded, they release moisture as precipitation (rain or snow), which returns to Earth. Then the cycle starts again. There is no new water— just the same water endlessly recycled by nature.

DEW DROPS ▶

The dew all over a spider web in the morning is the result of the water cycle. When the sun is out, warming the air, the air absorbs a lot of moisture. As the temperature falls in the night, the cooled-off air can't hold all that water anymore. The moisture "weeps" out of the air.

WHAT A DRIP!

Raindrops are not tear-shaped; they are round, with a little dent at the center. They are not made of just water: When water condenses, it collects around something. Often, a raindrop's core is a particle of dust, but a bit of salt, soot, or another tiny particle may serve the same purpose.

Raindrops range in size from a minuscule 1/50 of an inch to a relatively gigantic 1/4 of an inch.

TOO MUCH, TOO SOON

Heavy rain—in short bursts or longer downpours—can cause rivers to overflow their banks in a slowly rising tide or a sudden rush of water known as a flash flood. After a snowy winter and rainy spring in 1993, the Mississippi River and its tributaries flooded huge areas of land in the Midwest. It was the costliest flood in U.S. history.

TWO-TIMER

Most of the world has four seasons, with longer winters toward the poles and longer summers toward the equator. Many places close to the equator, however, have only two seasons: a rainy season and a dry season.

MUD

The ground can absorb only so much water. In hilly places, mud slides can occur. In 1969, a storm hit southern California with nine days of rain. That set off a series of mud slides, causing about $138 million worth of damage.

RAINY RECORD SETTERS

Mount Wai-'ale-'ale, on the island of Kauai, Hawaii, gets rain up to 350 days a year! Here are some other record setters:
• **Most rain in one year:** (August 1860–July 1861) 1,042 inches, at Cherrapunji, India
• **Most rain in one month:** (July 1861) 366 inches, at Cherrapunji, India
• **Most rain in one day:** (March 15, 1952) 73.62 inches, at Cilaos, Réunion (island in the Indian Ocean)
• **Most rain in one hour:** (June 22, 1947) 12 inches, at Holt, Missouri

▲ These people lost their home in a flood in Bangladesh.

FLASH AND BOOM!

A bolt of lightning is one of nature's most dramatic sights. Add the pounding of nearby thunder, and there's nothing like a lightning storm to quicken the heartbeat!

There are three types of lightning: cloud-to-cloud, cloud-to-air, and cloud-to-ground. Only about one fourth of all lightning hits the ground.

CHARGE IT

What makes the electricity that makes lightning? When a storm's fast-moving winds blow drops of water and bits of ice past each other, electrical charges build up. (It's something like the charge that builds up when you rub a balloon on your sleeve.) When a negative charge meets a positive, a current shoots between them: lightning!

BOOM

Thunder, which is the sound made by lightning, is created the same way as the sonic boom of a supersonic jet. Both the lightning and the jet travel faster than the speed of sound, which is 1,088 feet per second at sea level at 32°F. (The speed varies with altitude and temperature.) Lightning slices through the air so swiftly that it "breaks" the sound barrier—and we hear a boom.

COUNTDOWN

Count the number of seconds between the moment you see lightning flash and when you hear its thunder, then divide by five. The result is, more or less, the number of miles away the lightning struck. If you can't hear any thunder, the lightning is more than 20 miles away.

This splintered mess used to be a tree—before lightning hit it!

◀ STRIKE!

Lightning headed toward the ground takes the shortest route possible. That means whatever is highest above the ground is going to get hit. Don't get caught in the open, as the tallest thing around—and don't stand under the tallest thing (such as a tree). There is no time to run from lightning: It travels as fast as 90,000 miles per second!

The Vikings believed that thunder was mighty Thor throwing his hammer.

HOT STUFF

Lightning is one of the hottest things going: 54,000°F. That is more than five times as hot as the searing surface of the sun! Lightning is one of the major causes of forest fires around the world.

▶ Hailstones—water that has frozen, layer upon layer, into balls of ice—can fall during severe thunderstorms.

TWISTER!

Some thunderstorms go a step further and form tornadoes—the most violent of windstorms. The wind spins fast—to 300 mph—in a tight space and corkscrews downward.

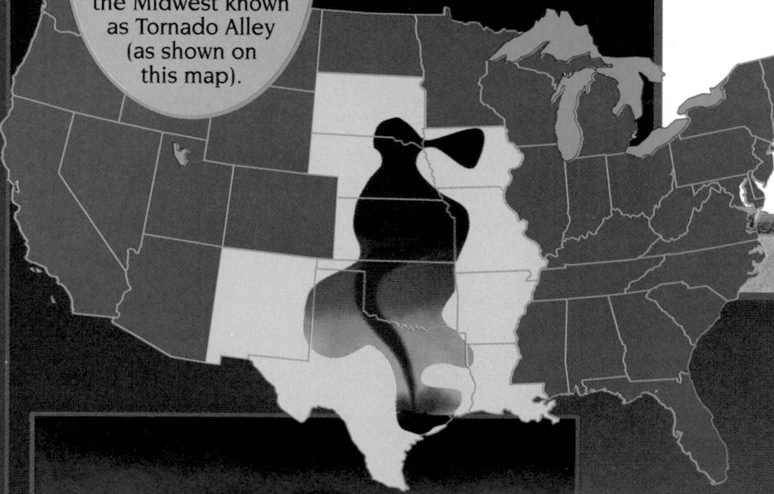

More tornadoes strike North America than anywhere else in the world. Most of those occur in an area of the Midwest known as Tornado Alley (as shown on this map).

A tornado's violent winds form a vacuum, and the tornado sucks up trees, houses, people, and animals as it passes over them.

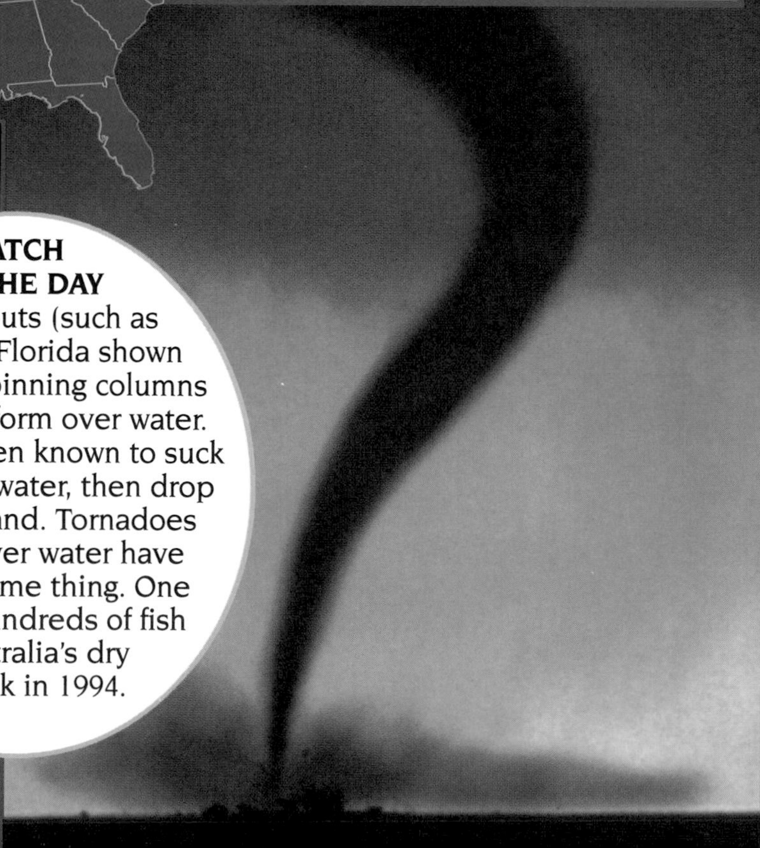

CATCH OF THE DAY

Waterspouts (such as the one in Florida shown at left) are spinning columns of wind that form over water. They have been known to suck fish from the water, then drop them over land. Tornadoes traveling over water have done the same thing. One dumped hundreds of fish on Australia's dry Outback in 1994.

AN UNWELCOME RECORD

The record for fastest tornado winds goes to a twister that struck Oklahoma on May 3, 1999. It was clocked at 318 miles per hour! That mile-wide monster stayed on the ground an unusually long time: nearly 90 minutes. It was one of 66 tornadoes that struck Oklahoma that day, killing 47 people. Thirty other twisters hit South Dakota, Nebraska, Kansas, and Texas the same day.

THE WILD BUNCH

Tornadoes usually occur in clusters, with many forming in the same day over a wide area. The deadliest such cluster struck on March 18, 1935, when tornadoes swept across parts of Missouri, Illinois, and Indiana, killing 689 people.

▲ DEADLY FORCE

A tornado's funnel is white at first, because it contains only water droplets. When it strikes the ground, however, it sucks up everything it touches, turning the funnel dark. The darker the twister, the more dangerous it can be. The debris trapped in its spin causes the worst damage: Powered by fierce winds, small pieces of rock, wood, metal, or glass slice through cars, buildings, and people.

Meteorologists follow tornadoes with high-tech equipment in the hopes of figuring out what makes these violent storms spin.

WHEN IT'S CHILLIN'

What's that cold stuff falling from the sky? Snow? Sleet? Most frosty forms of precipitation fall when temperatures drop to or below the freezing point.

THEY KNOW SNOW

The Inuit (IH-nuh-wut) people of Alaska, northern Canada, and Greenland—also known as Eskimos—have names for the many different types of snow. Where they live, knowing the differences can be a matter of life or death. Two of the names they use are:

* *pukak* (poo-KAK): snow that can cause an avalanche
* *mauja* (mow-YAH): deep, soft snow

▲ The above is a computer enhanced image of a stellar and plate combination snowflake.

WHAT A FLAKE!

It can take 100 tiny crystals of ice to form a single snowflake. Snowflakes are created when ice crystals move around in the air and stick together in amazing shapes. Meteorologists classify snowflakes into seven basic types: plate, stellar, column, needle, spatial dendrite, capped column, and irregular crystals. Each is formed at various temperatures and with different amounts of water. Many snowflakes are actually a combination of two or more types.

At this weather station on Mount Washington in New Hampshire, water droplets in the air (most likely in fog) have frozen on everything they surrounded. This white coating is called *rime*.

AVALANCHE! ▶

The avalanche may be the deadliest phenomenon of winter weather. It is a sudden slide of snow that plummets down a mountainside or off a cliff, burying everything in its path. This happens when a layer of new snow collects atop slick ice, or when sun warms a heavy layer of snow on a steep incline, making it just weak enough to tumble.

Almost anything—a shift in the wind, a sudden sound—can set off an avalanche. An avalanche can contain up to 100,000 tons of snow, be hundreds of feet wide, and tumble at 60 to 200 miles per hour. There is no outrunning one.

MORE, PLEASE!

Sometimes, Mother Nature doesn't make enough snow to please people—skiers and ski-lodge operators, for instance. So they make their own. Snowmaking machines work by cooling water to the freezing point (32°F), then spraying it high into colder air (below 32°F) to fall as snow.

PLOW NOW? AND HOW! ▶

When the wind in a snowstorm hits 39 miles per hour or higher, it's called a blizzard. One of the worst blizzards on record slammed the eastern U.S. on March 11-14, 1888. Up to 58 inches of snow fell, and some 400 lives were lost. In New York City, snowdrifts were high enough to cover second-story windows. This man is standing in a snow alley along Madison Avenue.

GREAT WHITE

Record-setting cold stuff around the world:

* **Coldest recorded temperature:** -128.6°F at Vostok, Antarctica, on July 21, 1983
* **Deepest snowfall in 24 hours:** 76 inches at Silver Lake, Colorado, April 14-15, 1921
* **Greatest snowfall in a single storm:** 189 inches at Mt. Shasta, California, February 13-19, 1959
* **Most destructive ice storm:** Damages worth $650 million in eastern Canada and northeastern U.S. in February 1998

CYCLONE!
People in the Western Hemisphere usually call them hurricanes, while people in the Eastern Hemisphere usually call them typhoons. Meteorologists call them tropical cyclones. Whatever you call them, they are powerful and deadly.

SPIN CYCLE
It takes warm water, lots of it, to make a tropical cyclone. If an ocean's surface heats up enough—to 80°F or higher—water rises in the air so fast that it starts to spin. The faster the spin, the more water is sucked into it, building a column of churning water with winds of more than 74 miles per hour. At the storm's center is a calm space known as the eye.

▼ Scientists aboard the space shuttle *Discovery* took this photo of Hurricane Elena in September 1985.

WALLS OF WATER
A tropical cyclone may be the most destructive storm on Earth. Besides torrential downpours, a cyclone's winds churn up walls of water 20 feet and higher. When these storm surges slam into coastal areas, they uproot trees, pound buildings and roads, and drown people and livestock.

FOLLOW THAT STORM!

By tracking a hurricane, meteorologists can predict where it will hit. Despite modern forecasting, however, disaster is not completely avoidable. In October 1999, an immense typhoon struck the eastern coast of India. More than 9,500 people perished as their villages were pounded by wind and washed away in the resulting floods.

This computer image tracks Hurricane Georges over 10 days as it made its way across the Caribbean Sea toward the southeastern U.S.

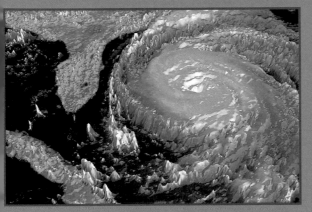

▲ Meteorologists use 3-D images of cyclones to analyze and predict their movements.

WATCH OR WARNING?

When a weather report includes a hurricane (or tornado) watch or warning, do you know the difference? A *watch* means that a severe storm could develop. You should follow the news for updates. A *warning* means that a severe storm has developed. Take shelter!

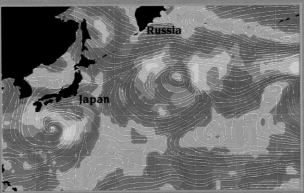

▲ Asia gets the lion's share of the 100 or so tropical cyclones that form each year—including these two typhoons off the coast of Japan. (The fastest winds, surrounding the eyes of the two storms, are in yellow.)

NAME THAT STORM!

The tradition of naming tropical cyclones was started in 1890, by an Australian meteorologist. Originally, he named them for politicians he disliked. Since 1979, both male and female names have been used. Hurricanes in eastern North America are named, in alphabetical order, from lists prepared by meteorologists from hurricane-path countries.

In 1995, wind and waves created by Hurricane Marilyn plucked these two sailboats from the water and deposited them in the neighboring parking lot.

WORKING WITH WEATHER

We couldn't ignore weather even if we wanted to. In fact, we look for ways to turn it to our advantage, first by trying to predict what is behind the next cloud.

▲ This thermometer also registers humidity, heat index, and wind-chill factor.

DO IT YOURSELF!

With practice, a sky watcher can tell a lot about approaching weather just by studying the clouds. Tools help, though. The handiest gauges include thermometers for temperature, barometers for air pressure, and hygroscopes for humidity.

AIR POWER

As air gets warmer, it rises. Hot-air balloonists know that and make it work for them. Heat the air just under the balloon, and up it goes! Want to come down? Let it cool. Balloonists also rely on wind—it carries them along, whichever way it's blowing.

SUPER SCANNER

Inside this dome is a Doppler radar antenna. It helps meteorologists track storm systems by telling them wind speeds and direction. Doppler radar also tracks precipitation: where it is, how heavy it is, and which way it is moving.

▲ UP, UP, AND AWAY!

Every day, twice a day, at the same times each day, some 500 weather balloons like this one are launched all over the world. They carry special instruments that detect levels of humidity as well as temperature and air pressure, and send them back as radio signals.

EYES IN THE SKY

Meteorologists use high-tech tools to help them study weather. In space, satellites beam down valuable data: air temperatures at various levels of the atmosphere, land temperatures, wind speeds, humidity levels, and radiation levels. They also send photographs of cloud patterns and storm movements.

A MOVING EXPERIENCE ▼

Sailors learn how to "read" the wind and use it to their advantage. Sails of different shapes and sizes have been designed to work with various speeds, strengths, and directions of the wind.

CATCHING SOME RAYS ▼

How is electricity generated where you live? Solar-power plants can generate power more cheaply than a fuel-burning plant—but only if they are built in places certain to get sunshine most of the year.

▲ These solar panels generate electricity at the world's largest solar-power plant, in the Mojave Desert, California.